POETRY
FOR MEN

Poems Across Three Continents

by
The Expiring Mind

Poetry For Men

Poems Across Three Continents

Copyright © 2017 by The Expiring Mind

All rights reserved.

ISBN: 1981682538

ISBN-13: 978-1981682539

POETRY

FOR MEN

Contents

Buttons, Buttons

Buttons, buttons
Buttons galore
I wonder
Just how many buttons there are?

We give such little thought
As it should be
When they are in place
But to lose one
Can be pure Catastrophe.

And try to match it
You will discover
Just how many there are
And not the same

Buttons of Brass, Wood and Bone
Plastic and Chrome
I wonder who invented the button?

And when I was a kid
And a friend did too
Tate, of all things to do

We collected buttons.

And to this day
Whenever we meet
With a huge smile
Past the years and the strife

He still says
Remember?
When we collected Buttons?
Ah yes... I remember it well.

Well they were cheap
We had nothing else
We got them for free
And they took us
All over the place

And people would ask us
What are you doing here
And we would say
Looking for buttons
Thought it was Obvious.

We would find them too
And thought we had found
The largest Diamond in the world
In the most unusual places.

Now, How did that get there?
I bet this button
Has a story to tell.

From a soldiers tunic
Or a Foreign clime
Little did I know how far
Looking for buttons would take me

I wish I had one
for each mile travelled
I'd have boxes and boxes

Buttons from Australia
Russia and India
Buttons from a Maharaja's chest
Arabia
And a Belly Dancer's vest

Just a pair of eyes and an ankle
Is all I remember
And lost in a Trance.

A camel train somewhere
What was that about?
Oh yes.
Looking for buttons.

Would I trade all my buttons

For a Dollar each
Heck no
Those dollars mean Nothing to me

I cannot do Those journey's again
I would have a button for each,
Memories, with each button
To sit and Reminisce
Two buttons for a friend I miss

One for him
And one for me
One of a Pair
And wonder Where
The Other one is.

Maybe, Someone will find it
And say
Now how did that get there?
I bet this button
Has a story to tell.

Life... It's all about Buttons you know.

Old Dead Tree

It's just an old dead tree.
It is, but not to me
It grew for maybe 60 yrs
Through rain and wind and weather,
Kinda, just like me.

And here it stands,
It's life all gone
But it's left behind this beautiful corpse
for birds to sit on.

I see the limbs all twisted and bare
And wonder if at all there's not
Something hidden there.
So we cut it down
And start to work.
My, Oh, My.
Once the bark is gone
That hid it from the world
It is a sight to behold.

It is twisted and knotted
Full of character, hard as a rock

And beautiful color.
Not life all gone
But just begun.
Just like me...

What Is In A Name?

They came long before you
Many, a long time ago
And as far as I can find
There are no monkeys
In my family tree.
Except, that is, for me.

For these were thoughtful
And rational men.
Not fashionable,
I would agree.
But thinking men
And they, a far sight
Smarter than me.

They built my framework
In which I reside
And these and no others
Will be the ones
To judge me.

If there's a life after this
Then these men will be there.

And they will be the ones
Who will ask me.
"What did you do with my name?"

They did not build machines
Like bicycles or cars and such
But these were the men
Who built the machines
That built the machines.
Like steam engines and steel.

They could work
To a thousandth of an inch
In complicated patterns
And this a hundred years ago.
And still in use today
Never to be improved upon.

These are the ones
Who will judge me
And say...
"What did you do with my legacy?
Oh dumb one,
You think it was all for free?"

Nothing

Nothing is a big thing
So let me explain

When you have nothing
Nothing is OK
You can give it all away
You have nothing to lose.

When you try to get something
Nothing is no good.
They gave me nothing
You will hear them say.
To keep what I've got
I'll give nothing away.

Until you have everything,
And nothing to gain.
No self worth
And mean
As mean can be.

I'm OK with nothing
Had it most of my life

Still got most of it left
After giving so much away.
Keep giving and giving
Can't seem to get rid of it all.

Nothing but Time
Trust, Advice, Friendship.
Loyalty, Humor, An ear,
A helping hand.
No payment required.

So much Nothing
Has been given
To me over the years
I don't know what to do with it all
Except give it away.

Makes sense to me
How about you?

Not Sad

Turn the lights down low
And let me sit here warm
By the fire
And let the tears freely fall

No, Not Sad
I just could not do it all.

Too much
Too much space
Too high to climb
Too far to race

Let me just sit here a while.

My Former Self

The old man cradled
The head of his dog
In his hands
As he had done
Many times before

And stroked the old grey head
And the tired eyes
Once more

Thank you he said
For the life
That we shared
And then the old dog
Was gone

Slowly
Using the back of a chair
The old man got to his feet
From the floor

His knees all shot
And his heart

As heavy as stone

What will become of me
Now he said
How do I go on alone?

I shamble along
And mumble some
Two brain cells
Stuck together by soap
And my only true friend
Now gone

As useless as a spent
Old cartridge shell
Just a shell
Of my former self.

Sure Kid

On the North Coast
Of Queensland
Where kids play in the surf.

Lives a Rip
That runs
Down the Beach

And quite unawares
Before anyone knew
Me and a kid
Were in its grip.

I can't swim too good
The kid said
As I struggled
To find a footing

That makes two of us
I thought
As I pulled him to my side
And we swam in tandem
Making no headway at all.

I could see the dire
Trouble we were in
In a huge bay
The rip curled
Out to sea

And I knew we
did not have the strength
To swim to shore
Even if the rip
Let us go

We'd not been missed at all
Just silently pulled away
While kids and parents
Still played on the beach
Of no help to us at all.

I thought then
we would drown together.
There was no way
I was letting him go
Neither one a help to the other
As we began to tire.

When my left foot
Hit a rock. A footing.
And in that instant

Judo flipped him
Over my hip
With the last of my failing strength.

He went over the rip.
Pulling me with him
And we lay spent
In the shallow water.

Saving him, saved me
I never let him go.
Thanks mister, he said
Sure kid.

The Mob

Seven men, trustworthy and true
All brothers, born of the same Mother.
Mother Earth and her brood
Of cattle, dogs and horses.

Four drovers, cook and wagon
Boss drover and horseman
To look after the horses.
Each drover had two horses
One for the night and one for the day.
Like people,
Some see better at night, than others.

No lariat, Not cowboys.
But stockwhips
On a long handle
Whirling and whirling
And then a sharp crack
Keeps the stock onward moving.

And Heelers,
dogs, well suited to the job
To drive on the mob.

Tough and as smart as they come.
You,
You could learn a thing or two.

No western saddles
No pommels needed
Stock saddles, to ride on all day.
The young,
Think this will be fun
But after a few hours, they're done.
Baked into the saddle
By the merciless sun.

The job is mighty
Worthy of a note
To move 18 thousand head
12 hundred mile
And requires
Everyone that's able.

And they come.
They come from far and wide
Stockhands with 20 horses and 20 dogs
And still it will take
Nine months
To move this mob.

And this not done
In a hundred years.

Could this still be done
Was there still pasture along the way?
Who knew?

And the ghosts of old drovers came
To show them the way.
The drovers all came
Their spirits released
To reclaim their heritage.
Clancy of the Overflow
And the Man from Snowy River.

On Brumbies,
The mountain horse
And every other breed
All lathered and sweating
They had been asleep.

They rode down the mountains
Their stockwhips whirling
Down the rivers and the valleys
Their yells blood curdling.
In all manner of dress
All tattered and torn
Never a more frightening
Scene to behold.
They had been asleep
For a hundred years.

And on they came...
Across the Tablelands
And beyond the Black Stump,
Their cries could be heard.
And the drum of the hoofbeats
Echoed into the night
Till they met with the herd.

The sound of the stockwhips
Still ringing in their ears
A sound like no other
And brings them to tears.

Whoosh, whoosh, whoosh
CRAAACK...
Whoosh, whoosh, whoosh
CRAAACK...
And a nip from the dogs
And the cattle were mustered.

And divided in lots
Eating as they go
Maybe, up to 10 miles a day.
Through dust and heat,
Through towns and over bridges.
These cattle that had never been driven...
They settle...
Now only 12 hundred
Miles to go.

And nothing stops them...
Except if they quit
But they don't quit, until it is done.
A mighty breed,
The Australian.

Hoping to Find

Looking to find
A home left behind
Where honesty
Was all I had

Hoping to find
A friend
To be true
As the friend
I left behind

Where sun shone
All day
The sun
I had never knew

Only to find
A Hole
In my heart
Where my home
Memories never grew.

Exiled

An ex-pat
From what
I'll never know.

With memories galore
That is for sure
And family and friends
That are true.

But for Custom
And Tradition
And a Home to Belong.
With sadness in my Heart
...All Gone.

Two Hands

Having just sprained a Wrist
I know you need Two hands
One for You
And one for the Ship

With sinews taught
And muscles straining
To pull in Wet canvas
In Waves and Winds shrieking

Blinded by Rain
Stretched over a spar
No shoes to deaden the feel
Of the Rope
That holds you
A hundred feet
Above the deck.

Just your Two Hands
To save the Day
One for You
And One for the Ship.

Work

If work is measured
In horsepower.
Then I'm glad
I'm not a Horse.

Cause, I don't like it
I've had my share
I can't say
I care much for it.

Grossly Over-Rated.

It is amazing to me
How simple a task can be
And yet take so much Work.

A thing of Beauty
Should create itself
But doesn't seem to be.
A Lifetime of Toil
To bring it Forth
Is what It takes.

Now me
Though work does not agree
When you see me working out
A Human Dynamo
Is what you'll see.

Powered by Purpose of Mind
And the Unrelenting Spirit
Of this big strapping Nurse

Phew... Glad that's over
Now, I can get back
To what I do best.

Planning my day
On the inside
Of my Eyelids
In a relaxing Pose
Fingers interlaced
On my Chest. Aaaaaaah

Bees

In four days winter will be here
And bees will not leave the hive.
But fan around the queen
To keep her alive

From the outside to the inside circling
And fanning their wings
To keep them warm
Eating the honey they have stored.

They say, if the bee
should ever disappear
Man would be extinct
By the 4th year.

So if you want to pray
Better pray, nothing should befall
These little workers
So overlooked
On which we depend for all.

Our Workaday Mind

In our workaday Mind
It's easy to forget
All that is offered.

And the poets
And Artists remind
Not to forget
That Beauty surrounds

Not about you or me
But Look and See

Not the thrill of the Ride
But the journey Inside

Not the changes we Made
But the changes we allowed
To take place
By the Generosity of Others.

A receiver am I
No gifts to Bestow
I can only pass on

What I am given

Some people have a Gift
It comes from Inside
And it is called
Peace of Mind

But not for me
It is not found
And I hide inside
My Workaday Mind

I Look and Look
And do not See
But you will
If you Close your
Workaday Mind

My Rocky Patch

What Does it Take? To make love germinate,
My gardener's thumb, Is stillborn.
In Rocky Barren, I try and try.

In one shower,
God can make, The desert bloom
And Millions come to see

But of my Rocky patch
God gave to me.
No one comes at all.

No Flower, or herb or fruit
To taste or smell.
Damn it, I think I will build
A Wall.

And when you come
Do you see?
The big old lump
Where no daisy
Grows at all

High, high up there
Do you see?
The Big Old Lump
By the Marble Wall.

That's me.

The Masterpiece

I knew a guy once
Made Grandfather Clocks.
An old guy
Lived down the street.

And as I drove by
With a casual wave
In his garage
He'd slowly be working.

I thought he was making
A couple of bucks
Like me.
I was wrong.

Why would anyone
Make a fine clock
When all that it did
Was tell time.
Like any old five dollar piece.

Now I'll tell you why
As you drive by

It would pay you
To stay alert.

Because that Old Guy
Is now me
And one day
With any luck
It might be you
Though that is not for certain.

So once I did stop
To say Hi.
And I asked him what.
He said Grandfather Clocks.

It was a mistake
An error of youth
Instead of what
I should have said
Why?

He'd acquired the skill
A craftsman he'd been
And had actually worked
The same place I did.

He was known there by all
As I asked around
And now I don't even

Remember his name.

But in someone's hallway
Stands a fine Grandfather clock
I should have begged him
To make me one.

I now would have paid
Any price at all
Because the skill and the love
he'd acquired are all gone.

But I had a family
And bills to pay.
I thought he was just
An old guy working away.

But what he left behind
For someone to adore
Not for me, too dumb
And too poor.
Was a work of art.

And he was just doing it
To pass the time.
For someone to admire
And make him feel proud.
The money didn't matter
And the hours he put in

He didn't mind.

So long as one person understood
And gave him the time.

And if it is you
You should be honored and thrilled
To see the finished
MASTERPIECE.

And he lived down the street
Just working away
Not bothering anyone
Just quietly working.

So I ask you
Give it some thought
Where do they make
Masterpieces these days
In what factory?!

The Record

I've gone thru the Record
And the Record shows
Boy, I spent a lot of Money
Last year.

And now the reckoning is due
Boy, I owe the Government too.
But it wasn't all for me
Though a lot of it was.

I helped out here and there
And made a Difference or two.
People helped me
I helped out too
Though maybe it wasn't to you.

It took a lot this year
To get me back on my feet
And for that I am Grateful.
In days gone by
I would have been dead - an End
To my life just like my Dad.

I dream and they come Alive
Just like they were here
I lean on their Strength
And go on from Here.
It doesn't all show
In the Accounting you know.

The Awakening

I awoke today from my slumbers
To the sound of dying embers
Where my dreams
Had gone up in smoke.

My financial advisor
He was complaining
He hadn't earned as much
This year.

But for me
He didn't care
That my cupboard
Was Bare.

I'd worked hard all year
I'd scrimped and I saved
To pay off
The debts that
I'd owed.

But I'd done it all wrong
According to him

And the bankers
Who had come before.

I should have multiplied my debt
And then I could afford
To Live
And pay double what it cost before.

If you think
They got away before
And you believe them now
Wait till you see
What they've got in store.

And of coarse
It is all my fault
It was me that caused all this.

I didn't spend enough
To their satisfaction
And paid off all my debt
From my meager pension.

Woe and betide me
When they come
A knocking
Don't I know

They can't afford
To live like this you know!

It's All In The Mind

I've been real lazy of late
I thought I was dead
But I ain't.

The ticker
Keeps ticking
But the brain
Is malfunctioning.

Where this leads
I haven't a clue
But we'll see
Soon as I get out of this chair
He, he.

I've lumber galore
Ten projects I know of
And many I don't.
Those I've forgotten
With any luck
Will soon be joined
By these others

And then I can sit
In my easy chair
With a clear conscience
And smile.

I've stacked my lumber
Sorted by thickness and length
All very pretty
I wonder what it was for?

I can calculate math
Like a wizard
Rho and beta
Gamma and theta
All 5 of the geeks
I mean greeks.

Oh dear there are only four
I wonder where the other one went.

Return on investment
That is a synch
Do I have an investment?
Beyond me.

I can hear you laughing
But I wouldn't
I might come live with you.

They say it's all in the mind
And I suppose it is
I just don't know where. Hehe.

Welcome To My World.

(Or... This one's mine, go get your own)

Oh, Lucky You
You may be
One of the very few
To ever read this Book.

It is only going
To be in print
Because of you
And the cold weather
In Oregon!

So, Take a Bow, Now.
A celebration of my Life
While I am still Alive
To enjoy it.

And now committed
To this Venture
Cannot back out
And will finally
Finish, What I started

After many Failures
Maybe to be Remembered
For what I did
And not for what I quit
And failed to do.

I thought some
Useful Chapters
Might be.

The Sun, The Sun
I know there is one.
Where is it?

I'm Black, I'm Black.
Yes, I was!

Invest your way
To Health, Happiness
And Catastrophe.

The Shambles
And The Pits
An area in Nottingham (not my life)

And

The Thirty-nine Steps

(That led to The Gallows)

I hope you will Enjoy!

Day 1

Do I LOOK OLD TO YOU?
It is the 2nd of January
I'm moving kinda slow
I'm washed and shaved
And writing this
Not for me
For you.

I'm off to breakfast...
It's 3 AM.
It has been a troubling night.
No Pain
Slept like a Babe in Arms.
But now I'm Awake
And Eager to get on
With the Day.

You can put this Tome
On your Kitchen Table
And when next you're
Having a Coffee
You can take
A sip from this as well.

I hope it will make you Smile.

The Danger is of coarse
You will warm to me.
It is not my fault
I didn't do it
It is Nothing to do with Me.

Or may Hate me.
Same Applies.

Day 2

I was raised in the 60's
On British Rock and Roll
"The British are Coming"
"The British are Coming"
Too Late
We're already here.

Via Australia.
A great country
You should go there
And Stay.
After all, you have put up with me
For all of 40 years.

Born in England
After the War
You had to make
Your Own Amusement.
And find your Humor
It was there
Just buried under Rubble.

Was there a Marshal Plan

For us. I don't know
All I remember
Is Free Milk
And me Lactose Intolerant
Or maybe it was to school
Either Way.
I didn't like it.

Enjoy my Life.

Nottingham

Me and water
I guess we are just
Not meant to get along.

To be a boy from Nottingham
I did not learn to swim
What were we going to swim in?

The Rivers and Canals were polluted
I felt sorry for the fish
When we caught them
I didn't want to put them back in.

Old cars and rubbish
Were thrown in the canals
You could almost walk across
On dry land.
There was so much
Rubbish and Filth.

And a local trip to the Ocean
To Skeggy
To Skegness

In the Height of Summer
You kept your Overcoat on.

Don't bother putting up
Your Brolly
To protect you from the rain
The howling gale
Will thwart you
And tear it from your hand.

But we fished the local river
The mighty River Trent
And in the winter
Full of Rain
And swirling Black
Would carry you down to the Ocean
Never to be seen again

On a November Day
And Freezing cold
By Newark Castle I cast
And somehow cast myself in.

My Dad upstream
Could only Look in Horror
But as I went Past
Tate (you will recall)
With a Fishpole in one hand
And a Ham sandwich

In the other.

Shoved the Ham sandwich whole
In his mouth and laughing
And Choking grabbed me by the collar
And hoisted me out before I drowned.

When I saw Him last
On his 70th Birthday
He still recalls that day
When Fishpole in One hand
And choking on a Sandwich
With Laughing
He pulled Me from The River.

Thanks Tate.

Now Think

Now think of your profession
What shoes do you wear?

A well dressed man
Starts with the shoes

Wingtips or Oxfords
Brogues all decorated
With patterns of perforations.

My Uncle Walt wore Boots
Black, thick Leather
That laced up over the Ankles
Made in Northampton
The Best they had to offer

And cost more than
A weeks wages.
Steel toecaps and Heels
To stop feet getting Crushed
Encased in supple leather
And polished.
Though you couldn't see that

Down the mine.

Double leather on the soles
Driven with Hobnails
To take the wear
For me to pull out and replace
When they were wearing low.

What kind of Profession
Wears out Boots made of Steel
And eventually the man inside.

You could hear them coming
A hundred strong
After the Whistle
Clumping on the cobblestones
Striking sparks from the hobnails.

They called them 'BOVER BOOTS'
Cos you didn't want any bother
From these.
"YOU WANT SOME BOVER?"
No, you didn't.

They sat in a place of Honor
By the fire
After all, it was these Boots
That had mined the Coal
From Down Below.

A Good One

This is a good One
You'll Enjoy this
But not as much as I did.

We never went Hungry
Not that I can Remember
But we might have come close
A bit.

I just didn't recognise it
Because it was often
I thought it was quite Normal

And the answer was always the same
What do you want for Tea?
(That's an evening meal to you)
We have Bread and Milk.

Bread and Milk?
Is that Normal?
To us it was
Have you had Bread and Milk?

The milk was heated in a pan
Careful not to scald it
And the white of the Bread added.
A choice!
Of a little Butter or Sugar
And there you have it.

Easy Peasy.
At least you can go to sleep
Without feeling you have
A sackful of kittens
In your stomach.

I wonder if it Tastes
As good as I remember?
I have some White bread
And some Milk.

PLUGHH! GROSS!

Looks and Tastes like Wallpaper paste!
With lumps in it.

Think I'll go get a Big Mac
Now, why weren't these Around
When I was a kid!

I Was Just A Kid

There were six hundred
Shops of all kinds
Butchers and bakers
Confectioners and grocers
Pubs and churches

Everything you can imagine
From the smells of the breweries
To the steam whistles of the factories
And the clop of the draft horses
Pulling the wagons

It was a hive
Of industry and people
Of cobblestone streets
And gas lighting
And houses
Row upon row upon row.

It had been the height of ambition
To bring workers
To where they were needed
To the Factories and Mills

The Mines and the Wharves
Because this was
The Industrial Revolution.

Now, with a hundred years
Of soot and grime
It was worn out
and in full decline.

But I was just a kid
What did I know?
With my arse hanging
Out of my britches.

There were lots of women with kids
A few even had dads
But a lot just had moms
It was all very sad.

There had been a war
Terrible but true
In fact there had been two
And the dads had all died
Leaving the women and the kids.

But what did I know
I was just a kid
With a dad.
They said 37 million had died

But nobody talked about it.

In my neighborhood
There were kids of all kinds
Polish, Irish and English
Catholic, Protestant and Jew
But mostly we were just
Ignorant, with dirty faces
And scuffs on our shoes.
Dirty knees and dirty hands
From playing around
The bombed out houses.

I learned as I went
And every day
Was a new adventure.
My friends to this day
Were Haydn and Tate, brothers
With me in age in the middle
What a threesome we made.

Tate was the oldest
And put me up
To all kinds of tricks
Which I passed down to Haydn.

Somehow though it was me
Who got the walloping.
But I didn't care

I was just a kid.
It only hurt a little bit.

I suppose we were poor
Or just working class
Which amounts to the same
But Honest and Truthful
When forced to it.

It didn't matter to us
Since we all had the same.
At least we weren't
Irish or Polish
Now those guys had it bad.
At least we could speak English.

The apple of my eye
Was Rita, her father was English
And her mother was Indian.
Her father had been a policeman
In India, and he had one eye
He could see right through you
And you didn't mess with him.

But we would sit and eat sandwiches
In her front room and watch telly
No one else was invited in.
She went to Catholic school
And was a ballerina

At least to me she was.

Her father must have thought me
The dumbest animal in town
Every day I'd knock on his door
And ask "can Rita come out and play?"
But he knew, one thing for sure
No-one was going to mess with Rita
Not while I was around.
I had fought every kid in town.

Rita was scared of dogs
And that's when I came into my own
Because my dad and Haydn's
Had German Shepherds
And no dog could intimidate us.
And we have the scars to prove it.

Bulldogs... they were the worst.
That is why my britches were oft
Ripped and torn and many a dog
went home shaking its head
From the whack that I give it.

Rita was Catholic
Mine was Anti
Anti Royalty
Anti Church
Anti Authority

Anti School

And our creed was
"Don't tell me what to do"
I hear that now sometimes
And I think hmmmm
I wonder how they came by that?

The City, in its wisdom
In order to redevelop the town
Made a new City Center
And our neighborhood
Would be torn down

So slowly, year after year
Neighbours disappeared
And so did the houses
And one by one the shops closed down

To us it was cruel
Our favorite
The candy shop was gone
And no longer was I needed
To protect Rita from barking dogs
As we walked along.

Then family began to move
A whole bus ride away
You'd need a bicycle to get there
Only grandma stayed.

Then when she died
They boarded up the house
And now all the shops were gone.
So too were the factories
No throngs of workers
All moved miles away.

They built new houses
But who these people were
I had no idea.
My dad got a new house
And we too moved
My childhood was gone
And so were Haydn and Tate.

If shops determine
A community
And there were
600 before
When they had finished
Rebuilding. Now there were
Only 4.

I wonder what
The new kids
made of that.
But they were just kids
What did they know?

My Dad

Today I go to work out
Not for muscle tone
But to get this old heart restarted
It really is a drone.

But who knows
Someone may need
A few minutes of this old heart
Otherwise it doesn't seem to be
A lot of use to me.

I take from life my share
And put back where I can.
I think this heart has been here before
I think it was in my dad.

Everywhere I go these days
I see my dad somewhere
I look down at my hands and say
I didn't know my dad was here!

He sure did put up with a lot.
He had to put up with me

And when he'd had enough, he said
"Here's a ticket to Australia,
See if you can find your way back!"

My dad had a heart of gold
So if by chance I have it
It's OK with me.

The Scotsman

A short sharp shrill
Pierces the morning air
And wakes you from
Your slumbers

And shatters
The rain and cold
On your windowpane.
It is still dark outside.

Hot metal smells
Like a sweating horse
And sits sweating and shaking
All black and shiny
Then gives a tremendous snort

Muscles of steel
And rods for arms
And legs
Made of wheels.

Take up the strain
And the wheels

Begin to turn.

With lungs of fire
And nostrils wide
Belching smoke and ash
High in the air.

Workers in the field
Fork and hoe in hand
Stop and stare.
Mesmerised.

And pride beats
In their hearts
And they take off
Their caps and cheer.

A mighty force
Is on the move
And pushing through the air
On rails of steel.

That traverse the earth.

High steel wheels
Turning fast
The fastest thing
On Earth

The fireman
Shovelling fast
With the firebox door
Wide open, lights the
Engineer at his task.

To make this
360 ton of iron, steel and brass
Be the fastest in the world.

And a giant great caterpillar
Of black green and gold
Of engine and carriages
Shakes the ground
As it goes thundering past.

'The Flying Scotsman'
Steam locomotive
The fastest in the world.

The Greatest Show On Earth.

Whisperings

With faint whisperings
Of memories past
That echo in my brain

My childhood
And my youth
Are reborn
They were not so bad.

But come listen
The story has not ended...

The Scotsman
After many years
Was finally decommissioned
And replaced with some
Diesel Electric MONSTER.

Yes, it could go faster
But who cared
No steam whistle
To separate you
from your dreams

And finally we stopped listening.

It languished broken
In some scrapyard many years
But was rescued by a doctor
Who bought it.

But the plan did not work out
It was too soon
And it went to a museum of steam
Where it sat for many years.

Then with fresh paint
And loving care
It was put on display
And we could visit
On a rainy day.
And wonder
Boy, those were the years.

But Now
Do You Hear?
What you have not heard before?

REBORN, REFIT
TO PLY THE RAILS
FROM LONDON TO YORK
IF ONLY THE DOCTOR COULD SEE THIS.

And passengers line up
To get on
And say they rode
'THE FLYING SCOT'

One day before too long
I must have a ride on it
So I too can say
I RODE THE FLYING SCOT.

CAN YOU LOVE?
IRON STEEL AND BRASS?
YES, YES YOU CAN!

Australia Bound

Life in the Sixties
Was Grim
Unless you were in
A Rock and Roll Band
And your name
Was The Rolling Stones

The Choice was few
And the employers Knew
They offered work
But the Tasks
Were repetitive and Boring

Or go down the mines
To die a daily death
Of no sun.

You could work
For Raleigh or Players
Making bicycles or cigarettes.
But I chose none of These
I had had my First love
And I Loved Motorcycles.

You were in the Wind
And Free
And little be known
I had an Understanding
Of how they worked
And to go as fast as could be.

I think I had inherited it
From my Grandpa and his brother
Who made Lace Machines
And could work
To a Thousandth of an inch

But the Industry was Dying
The air set you Crying
The River polluted
And the Green Hills
Were covered with Coal

Bugger this,
I am Australia Bound.
Where the sky is blue
The water is bluer.
And the Sun shines
All Year.

I was ignorant
Of the Spiders and Snakes

Box Jellyfish And Sharks
Or the Criminals
That had founded the place.

What did I care
I was a kid Again.

A One-way Ticket

Life was Harsh
And Childhood
Ended Early.
And if you were caught
With Trap and Snare
On the Dukes
Local Estate.
You could expect no mercy.

A trip to Australia
Was not the vacation
It is today.
With your wife and Family
Left behind.
To work in the Mines
Digging for Coal
Up to your Neck
In Saltwater.

It would be a Release
A Reprieve.
To have this Servitude
End Early.

By Mutual Consent
To have your Life end
At the Hands of the Man
Chained behind you.

All for your Crime
Of feeding your Family.

A New Life

Born in England
All pale and Wan
And arrive in Australia
The First thing you ask
Is Phew!
Where did that Sun come from?

From Pale to Mahogany
Your skin changes color
Prisoner of Mother England
Or POM for short
You are no longer.

You'll adopt a Twang
And the vowels change too
And everything is said in a question?
FAIR DINKUM!

Your eyes narrow to slits
You'll wear shorts and boots
Over your ankles.
When it rains you'll take your socks off
And when it stops

Put 'em back on again.
Hate wet socks.

The dust all red
Covers everything
And you'll wear a hat.
Some have bottle corks dangling
From the brim
To help keep flies
Outta the eyes.
It is all very Scientific!

When working near water
You'll keep an eye open
For Crocodiles and Snakes.
Don't go in long grass
Might not come out again.

Working on fences
To keep the cattle in
From getting stuck in the river
Where they sink and drown
And a bugger to get out.
So keep the fences Tight
And properly done
Should twang like a Harp.

You are all Mates
And help one another.

This is me 'mate'
You'll introduce one to another.
He's from Ol' England
But he's all right
And then you're accepted
As Australian.

All immigrants
But all belong.

Though I must say
it is hard on the women folk
It is miles and miles
To the stores.
But it's easy to remember
They all have the Same Name.
Sheila... That's it
Easy... All the same.

Barramundi

Barramundi is a wonderful fish.
Like a Salmon in reverse
Born in the Ocean
Before going in the Rivers.

You find it where Freshwater
Meets Saltwater.
Where Rivers meet the Sea.

Unfortunately,
Crocs like them too.
That's Crocodiles to you.
And in Northern Queensland
There are plenty of those!

A bright Moonlit night
Really, early Morning
About 2am.
We are going for Barramundi.
Rowing down a River
Heading out to Sea.

In a row boat

with no motor
How crazy can you be?

The Moon is shining bright
And we are just rowing along
When suddenly The Moon went out.
Completely.
It was as black as it can be.

What happened to the Moon?
I asked. And Nevin said
Row! Row, like there is no tomorrow!
And turned the boat around.

I could not figure it out
How come the moon went out?
And now we were rowing like Mad.

And Then the Rain came down.

It threatened to fill the boat
And while Nevin was rowing
I was Bailing.
Now I understood
Stormclouds had covered the Moon
And now we were in it good.

Out in the Ocean.
In a row boat, with no motor!

How he knew where to go
I do not have a clue,
I could not see a thing.
I just kept on Bailing
I learned to pray, that day.

We rowed right past
Sleeping Crocs
And up the River.

We couldn't get any wetter.

We tied up at the launch site
Get in the car he said
So I did and started to dry off.
With a towel, I found in the back.

I wondered where he was
He was just taking so long
I thought a Croc had got him.
Him standing by the water so.

Finally, a Knock came at the Window
And I rolled it down.
The storm came in, it was pouring down.
What are you doing he asked?
I'm standing out here holding the boat
Waiting for you to bring the car!

Among many other Expletives,
About me being a POMIE So and So.

I thought you said
Go get in the car
I piped to no avail
The water pouring down
Washed my voice away.

We sat in stoney silence
The rest of the night
While the rain came down
And the engine running.
We slowly steamed ourselves dry.

It was a long drive home.

Great fish Barramundi.
If you can get one.
It took along time to live that down.

Cricket

I don't feel at home Here
No, I Don't.

I am not an Immigrant
I was merely on Loan

With strange ideas
Of what's Right
And what's Not.

THAT'S... Not Cricket
You Know!

Not bloody Done
Don't you know
Not Right
Not Proper
A tad Underhand
Self Serving
Simply not done.

Have you not noticed
All the Countries

That play Cricket
Jolly good show

India, Australia and Canada
But not the USA.
I wonder why that is?

They finally caught on to soccer
A little bit.
And play in a World Series
All by Themselves

The rest of the World
I guess don't count.
So, I don't feel at Home here
No, I don't
And if you Ask me Why.

I'll Tell you
You don't play Cricket
FOR A START!

Two Lives

I have two Lives
One down here
In quiet Sophistication
In shorts and tennies
Sipping Pimm's

And the Other
In Oregon
Trying to lure
A Mackinaw Trout
Or big Brownie
(Without much success)

Friends in Both
A surprise to say
Who both seem
Equally pleased to see me
(Don't know why)

Maybe it's my dog
They really like
And they just
Put up with me.

I really would like
A cabin by a Lake
Close enough to throw
A line in from my front door.

I'd tie a little bell
On it to hear it ring
Over the sound
Of sizzling Bacon.

With a day Bed
And wood burning Stove
To keep the Kettle boiling.
I love a Cuppa.

But when the weather
Drops to One degree
I don't care what you
Measure it in

California is a pretty good place to be.

Just Too Full

I came right home
And fell asleep.
A sign of a clear conscience
Or, just too much alcohol

Anyway, In my dreams I remembered
What my heart surgeon
Had said to me.

So I am going to
Repeat it to you
But in strict confidence of coarse.
I don't want people to think I'm nuts
But it's OK for you to.

When they opened up my chest
The heart was in pretty good shape.
They thought they could use it again
But when they looked inside
They found all manner of junk.

Dogs galore,
A motorcycle or two

And even a Jaguar
A beautiful XK140.

As they cleared out all of this rubbish
It became apparent there was something
Quite unusual here.

It was a chasm
A thousand mile wide
From East to West.
That had been filled
Right to the brim.

With poets and stories
Of dreams and hopes and regrets
And pains of loves lost
Memories of long ago.

They packed it all in storage
And gave me a catalog.

Then said.
You may seem
Quite empty at first
With echoes and noises
that will seem like voices.
From the past.

We recommend you keep it in your head.

That's hardly been used at all
And not in your heart.
Your heart was just too full.

So with an empty heart,
Seems strange, I can go on my way.
But my brain, that has never been so good
Because I've already decided.

I am going to
fill it, all up again.
With memories and moments
Too precious to forget.

With travels and journeys
And dreams of fireside nights
Of dinners and good company.
Laughs and jokes
Music and poems
And people
I love the most.

And so today... I think I will.

The Short Version

I'll keep this short
Now don't get me started
I'll stick to what I know.

This morning in the pouring rain
I went for my usual breakfast
I thought I was in OREGON

At 5am in a line at a 24 hr
Donut shop. My favorite.
Mine the only white face in line
That time of the morning.

That's OK
I was an immigrant too
And I never had a problem
Not like a few I could mention.

Always respectful
To my face and my back
Not the people but the Politics
That's crap.

I don't understand How
The richest person in the World
Is of all things... Mexican.

Carlos Slim
He must be smarter
Than us all combined.

I won't get into politics
My blood pressure
Won't stand it
Both sides of the border

One dirty hand
Washing the other
And the people caught
In the middle.

Where ever you look
It is all the same
Europe or the Middle East
We look to politics
To set our fate.

Good luck with That
You should check their track record

Thanks but no thanks
I think I will choose

My own Fate.

There I'm done.
And my coffee is cold
NOW... you got me Mad.

A Tale of Two Faces

Here's a little ditty
To peruse
While sitting
In the Privy

Written on the back
Of a contract
It is better that
Than the other alternative.

All Corporate Blackhole legalese
Minus the conscience of a reasonable Man
Or the blessing of State Law

I have loved this place
My second home
My kids and Grandkids live here.

And I get to escape
For the summer at least
Crazy California

But this year a black cloud hovers

After making plans all year
To find without any warning

When to pay the rent
If you want to stay here
As the past 4 years
The rent has nearly doubled
And more to come.

I wouldn't mind at all
If some of that windfall
Would benefit the workers here
Who rescue my dog
and serve me coffee
Each morning with a cheery smile

But probably goes to a Corporate Bonus pool
For some cretin who meets his goal.
They must be from far away
I've never met that here.

And this is what they say
We have people waiting in line
And if you can afford to go to Italy
You can afford to pay.

That is the rationale now
So beware
There will be more next year

But me, I won't be here.

But don't be fretting over me
I'll be in Italy
In Olive groves and grape
Carving Marble.

There is always somewhere else
And people worthy to meet
Who don't follow
A hollow Corporate Creed.

Did Ya Miss Me?

Did ya Miss me?
Probably not
With all the commotion.

I chose not to compete
And instead was planning
My vacation

Vacation? From What?
I am so overworked
I can Hardly find time
To get out of Bed.
I need some Motivation.

But did you notice
Or just Distracted
That the Drought is over
And the ducks can swim
In LA Arboretum
Instead of just walking around

The Farmers can plant
And get back to work

And the Weeds
Will take over my place.

The driveway to shovel
From the mud washed down.
The dog to walk
And the House to paint

And all this before
I can get out of Bed.
Boy, I need a vacation.

It ain't a Poem

What makes a Poem?
I don't know
I only hope
It don't have to Rhyme

So this is a poem NOT
More of a complaint.
They said it was going to Rain
It did and brought my ceiling down

A flashing had rotted out
I had to take the siding off
To let it all dry out
So now it is all dried out
And I got the ceiling back

Hold on, of coarse it couldn't wait
For me to fix the leak
Before they scheduled rain again.

So with bright blue Tarps
My house is covered
To protect my brand new Ceiling

But now they forecast High Winds
And my tarps wont stand up to that
So now my House is covered in Blue Tarps
And 4x8 sheets of plywood

I feel like I am in The Ark
I don't think there were windows in that either
But I can guarantee
This one definitely won't float.

No wonder I wasn't asked to build The Ark
Cos it would not have been ready
And Over Budget.

Meanwhile the rain is pouring down.
!@##$%%&**... JUST IN TIME!

Where to Find Me

Tomorrow I begin
A new
Cardiovascular Regimen
To finish
What I started
Up in Oregon

With Nurses
Oh, so Pretty
And a doctor
Oh, so Grim

Not on a Bicycle
Made for two
On a Bicycle
Made for One

Then a fast...ish
Walk, around a Track
Before flexing muscles
On my back.

What A Stud.

Wednesday - That's a Good Day

Monday, Tuesday... EXERCISE
Thursday... EXERCISE
Yes. Now you see
Wednesday is a good Day
No exercise for me.

So now I'll write this Poem
Do you see the Time?
3:55. That's AM
I am washed and shaved
And heading out to Breakfast
While you're Still fast asleep

When I get back
There's weeds to spray
A roof to fix
A van still to convert to an RV
Thank goodness
There's no exercise today
For Me.

So why am I exercising
When energy I have

None to Spare?
To come home exhausted
And the Afternoon asleep!

Why. So I can do
The things I Love
Be with the people I like
Except I am too damn
Busy sleeping
And catching up on Chores.

Too much exercise
To my way of Thinking
Should be regulated
Like too much Sugar and Salt
And used only
When Absolutely needed.
It is not good for your Health.

But... Today is Wednesday
And it is a good day for me.

I Don't Understand it

I don't Understand
Would someone explain
Why
People do this to themselves.
And say it is fun.

Only my second day
And already I'm done
To fall into bed
Still with my boots on.

At least tomorrow
There is no workout for me
I'll unlace my boots then
And the dog can just
Walk by herself.

Me...
I plan to get drunk.
Inebriated, sloshed, pickled.
Cos on Thursday
It starts all over again

They say it is good for me
And make me live longer
They say while drinking coffee
And me chained to a treadmill!
Don't they Know
How Old I am?

Why! Why would I want
To live Longer?!

Another Day

Surely, surely
Not Really.
Really?

Can this be True
With just a few
More pages to Fill

One after Another
My pens
Are run dry.

Should I bother
To buy Another?

The eyes are all Bleary
The image is Vague
Maybe better this way
Than bring into view

A harsh Reality
To put on my Glasses
And look in the Mirror

And first thing
In the Morning too

Surely, surely
This can not be True.
Another bloody day
And a workout too!

Oh, by the way
Happy Valentines to You.

Beat That

Why cannot I find
A girlfriend,
To be honest.

More like
My dog?

Two brown adoring eyes
And a smile from ear to ear.

Of fashion or furs
She has no need or desire

One meal a day
She is cheap to keep.

And I get to watch
Any movie I choose.

And everyday
I tell her the same

You are so pretty

And she'd crawl on my lap

If she could
A few pounds ago.

Without a murmur
Just a head on my arm

Two brown eyes
Tell me it's time

To go for a walk.
Don't you know
It's raining and cold outside?

She waited all day
For this one thing
To go for a walk
With her Master
Her friend
Who she would defend
To her very last Breath

And all
For an absentminded pat
An ear tug
Or a belly rub.

Beat that.

I Drink Only Beer

Here I sit with Broken wing
As pretty as a Bird
But unable to Fly
And I cannot tell you Why

Suffice to say
If you decide to come visit me
The pots pile high
In the kitchen sink
And I
Only drink Beer.

The reason is Simple
You'll understand
Way back in London
The word 'Plague' was heard

They thought it was caused by bad air
And I guess they had lots of that
But armed only with paper and pencil
A young doctor went in

And drew a map of all the houses

And the ones with plague
He marked with an X
The worst was around a water pump
In the street so now he knew.

It was not bad air
But bad water and the disease
Was CHOLERA

Of one area he noted
Was no Disease at all
Around the local Brewery
The people there did not drink water
They only drank Beer

And boiled for Brewing
Killed the disease
So there you have it
I only drink Beer

DON'T WANT TO GET CHOLERA!

I Love DVDs

I love DVDs.
My kids say
The more boring
The better.
It is true.

I love movies
They give us a life
We never knew.
Someone else's.

We can roam
Thru outer space
Or back in time
Or better yet
To a country
We've never been.

What is more
We can understand
Ourselves much better
Or for worse.

And realise that
Our own life story
Has worth.
Maybe
They will make a movie
Of yours.

Just One More Day

Just one more day
Is all I ask
To see it through
From first to last

For tomorrow is the longest night
And the shortest day.
And I know where I'll be
At 5:45 am.

To celebrate
In good old pagan style
With Holly Berry
And Mistletoe
The end and the beginning.

And the sun
Does halt it's retreat
And will begin again to ascend.

Knowing this
And a warm fire
Makes three months

Of winter
A little easier to take.

So take a minute
And walk your garden.
See where the line is
Between dark and light

And mark the spot
Of the longest shadow
No further will it go
And day by day
It will recede
Turning dark into light.

And so begins again
The story of life.
See if it isn't so.

Failure

Failure is the only success I've had but it has not all
    been in vain.
I've learned a lot along the way and made many
    friends
Some I've even managed to keep and I am always
    on the lookout for new ones.
Especially, if I think they can benefit from my vast
    array of experiences.
To list a few.
Gardener... failed.
Sculptor... failed.
Poet... failed.
Alcoholic...
My kids... Thankfully, they just laugh.

Too Much

Too much
Too, too much
Too much has Passed

Too much Time
Too many Years
Too old Now
Too few to Go

Too many Aches
Too many Pains
Too Cranky
Too much Impatience

Too much to Do
Too many Cares
Too many Tears

Too much Butt
Too short of Breath
Too short in the Leg

To Want to get on that BIKE.

Now- Get out of the Way
And Watch Me Go.

Who Knows What

What force is this
That powers me on
To rage on thru the night
And illuminate
My wild imaginings

And in the morning
To set about the tasks
To bring these thoughts to life
And to reach beyond my abilities

And then to watch
Them slowly wither and die
Spent in the sunlight
Under a critical eye
Of disappointment

All gone
Consumed on an altar
To what God, I do not know
One day of life.

To leave my portion

A smoldering ember
Just one small part
From which to start anew

I Thank You

I thank you
For your kindly attention
You have put up
With a lot I know

But I think I have reached
My limits of Invention
Though I could go on and on

What I write has been to the
Benefit of the writer
To exorcise demons you know
But I hope they struck
A chord or two.

Your kindness probably saved
Someone becoming an alcoholic
Long dark nights
And long dark mornings.

Give too much time
For reflection
It had to go somewhere.

And the dog
Has heard it all before.

I hope to find pastures new
Get in shape
And ride my bicycle
On summer balmy nights

So I bid you Adieu
It was fun.
Who Knew.

The expiring mind...expired.

* * *

Printed in Great Britain
by Amazon